WESTERN CIVILIZATION! THE COMPLETE MUSICAL (abridged)

book and lyrics by
Reed Martin & Austin Tichenor
original music composed by
Nick Graham
additional material by Dee Ryan

BROADWAY PLAY PUBLISHING INC
224 E 62nd St, NY NY 10065-8201
212 772-8334 fax: 212 772-8358
BroadwayPlayPub.com

WESTERN CIVILIZATION! THE COMPLETE
MUSICAL (abridged)
© Copyright 2002 by Nick Graham, Reed Martin, and
Austin Tichenor

All rights reserved. This work is fully protected under the copyright laws of the United States of America. No part of this publication may be photocopied, reproduced, stored in a retrieval system, or transmitted, in any form or by any means, electronic, mechanical, recording, or otherwise, without the prior permission of the publisher. Additional copies of this play are available from the publisher.

Written permission is required for live performance of any sort. This includes readings, cuttings, scenes, and excerpts. For amateur and stock performances, please contact Broadway Play Publishing Inc. For all other rights please contact the authors c/o B P P I.

Cover photo compliments of Reduced Shakespeare Company

First published by B P P I in September 2002
This edition: November 2016
I S B N: 978-0-88145-682-0

Book design: Marie Donovan
Assistant to the Publisher (2002): Michele Travis
Copy editing: Sue Gilad
Page make-up: Adobe InDesign
Typeface: Palatino
Printed and bound in the U S A

WESTERN CIVILIZATION! THE COMPLETE MUSICAL (abridged) was originally produced and performed by The Reduced Shakespeare Company under its original title THE COMPLETE MILLENNIUM MUSICAL (abridged). The first public performance was on 20 October 1998 at the American Stage Festival in Nashua, NH. In November and December 1998 it was performed at the University of Alaska at Anchorage, the Pier One Theater in Homer, Alaska and the Pittsburgh Public Theater. It opened at the Kennedy Center in Washington, DC on 5 June 1999 for an eight-week run, followed by a successful season at the Edinburgh Fringe in August 1999 and the Israel Festival. Later that year it ran for six weeks at the Seattle Repertory Theater. Three separate companies then began touring the United States, Great Britain, and Australia simultaneously.

The original cast and creative contributors were:

> Reed Martin
> Dee Ryan
> Austin Tichenor

Directors ....Reed Martin & Austin Tichenor
Musical director/arranger...............................Nick Graham
Technical director... Daniel Kays
Costume designer..Sydney Wellen
Lighting & scenic designer ....S L Wellen
Choreographer... Amy Moorhead
Props ....Nicole Donery

SPECIAL THANKS

For their contributions to the development of the script, the authors wish to thank Adam Long, Matt Croke, Dan Kays, Zach Moore, Amy Moorhead, S L Wellen, Sydney Wellen, Nicole Donery, April Nickell, American Stage Festival (Nashua, NH), Michael Barnhart, Megan Dick, Christi Graham, Rachel Hamilton, Daniel Hurwitz, Russell Lees, Jane Martin, Pier One Theater (Homer, Alaska), Pittsburgh Public Theater, Joan Pohlhammer, the Sebastiani Theater (Sonoma, CA), John Tichenor, and the University of Alaska, Anchorage.

IMPORTANT NOTE

The name "Reduced Shakespeare Company®" is a Registered Trademark, and its use in any way whatsoever to publicize, promote, or advertise any performance of this script is EXPRESSLY PROHIBITED.

Likewise, any use of the name "Reduced Shakespeare Company®" within the actual live performance of this script is also EXPRESSLY PROHIBITED.

THE PLAY MUST BE BILLED AS FOLLOWS:

WESTERN CIVILIZATION!
THE COMPLETE MUSICAL (abridged)

book and lyrics by Reed Martin and Austin Tichenor

original music composed by Nick Graham

additional material by Dee Ryan

FOR WHAT IT'S WORTH

Although we use the names Austin, Dee, and Reed within the script, each cast member should use his or her own name when performing the show.

There are a number of topical references in the script. The humor and relevance of these will fade over time, so we encourage each production to change these references to keep them as up-to-date as possible.

The production elements described in the script are from the original production by the Reduced Shakespeare Company. Consequently, the scenery, props, and costumes were all "reduced" in both quality and number. You will not be so encumbered, and may be tempted to use real explosions, live animals, and leggy showgirls. This sounds like fun, but may falsely raise audience expectations.

Finally, even though it's a musical, try to keep the campy elements to a minimum. Play it straight. Keep it moving. Many of the punchlines are meant to be throwaways. And for those of you who think the whole script should be thrown away, we can only say we tried that, and it didn't work nearly as well.

ACT ONE

(Dramatic music begins and the lights fade to black. A light rises on each person as they begin to sing.)

AUSTIN: The future is now, so we have the chance

DEE:
To show you war and tragedy—in song and dance!

REED: We'll learn the ways both good and bad
The western world has grown

ALL: And then we'll find out all the things
We've never really known…

(Heavy disco beat. Wah-wah guitars. Mirror ball. They shimmy and groove like it's 1977.)

AUSTIN: We'll tell you some facts

REED: Some old and some new

DEE: We'll cram a thousand years into an hour or two

AUSTIN: And when it's all over you will have to agree

ALL: History ain't what it used to be!

REED: We'll tell you a joke

AUSTIN: We'll sing you a song

DEE: We'll get everything right

ALL: Except when we're wrong

REED: We'll tell you the truth, it'll set you free—

ALL: History ain't what it used to be!

AUSTIN/DEE: History ain't what it used to be!

REED: We'll be turning history inside out

AUSTIN/DEE: History ain't what it used to be

REED: Upside down and roundabout

(Eight bars of dance)

REED: If you've seen us before

AUSTIN: You know the drill

DEE: It's the same old jokes

AUSTIN/REED: But we added a grill!

DEE: *(Spoken)* Girl!

REED: His name is Austin!

AUSTIN: He's Reed!

DEE: I'm me!

ALL: And history ain't what it used to be!

(Music continues. AUSTIN and DEE dance, while REED speaks.)

REED: Ladies and gentlemen, we are gathered here this evening to examine our past. Tonight you'll learn all about the history of Western Civilization. And how better to start the show than with the single greatest musical style that civilization has yet produced—Disco!

AUSTIN/DEE: History ain't what it used to be

REED: We'll be turning history inside out

AUSTIN/DEE: History ain't what it used to be

REED: Upside down and roundabout

(Four bars of dance)

AUSTIN: I done my research

DEE: Got my degree

ACT ONE 3

REED: We wrote some great numbers
My favorite was three

ALL:
'Cause if we forget what happened way back when
We're doomed to repeat it over and over a—
Over and over a—
Over and over a—

AUSTIN/DEE: History ain't what it used to be!

REED: Turnin' history inside out

AUSTIN/DEE: History ain't what it used to be!

REED: Upside down and roundabout.

ALL: *(Spoken)* History!

DEE: Thank you. Thank you very much.

REED: Good evening ladies and gentlemen. Welcome to the _____ Theater and tonight's performance of WESTERN CIVILIZATION! THE COMPLETE MUSICAL *(abridged)*.

AUSTIN: Tonight, you'll witness the unthinkable—the entire history of Western Civlization in a single evening.

DEE: We will take you from the Dark Ages to the Information Age.

AUSTIN: From the abacus to the computer.

REED: From Beowulf to Baywatch.

DEE: We've come so far, haven't we?

AUSTIN: Yes, we have, and tonight you'll get it all. How the development of Western Civilization hinges on the great turning points in history, many of them triggered by the great visionaries you've all read about. Galileo, Wilbur and Orville Redenbacher, Sigmund Freud. All the great thinkers. And the development of the world's great Art. Like Disco!

DEE: No, disco sucks.

REED: Especially the way we do it.

(Ideally, any latecomers should be getting to their seats now so that the harassment can begin. It should go something like this:)

AUSTIN: All right fine, then other great inventions... *(Noticing the latecomers)*...like the invention of the watch!

REED: *(To the latecomers)* It's all right. I don't think anyone noticed.

DEE: *(To the latecomers)* Where were you?

(Go after them. Get a real answer. If it's something like "We had trouble parking" or "We were having dinner" or "Too much traffic", AUSTIN *should say:)*

AUSTIN: Oh, I see. Did anyone else drive/have dinner before the show?

(When most of the audience raises its hands)

AUSTIN: Gee, and yet somehow...

REED: Oh, "having dinner"! *(Or whatever)*

(They all mime drinking. If it's a couple of kids who are late, you can mime smoking a joint. Then REED *can say:)*

REED: You'll be happy to know they sell snacks during intermission.

(Or sometimes [but not always], the excuse can be made to sound like a euphemism for sex. In which case:)

REED: Oh, "having dinner"! *(Or whatever)*

DEE: Is *that* what they're calling it now?

REED: They do look a little disheveled. Just a reminder: no smoking in the theatre.

(Don't go on too long. Just enough to get some information you'll need later and to let the audience know you'll be

ACT ONE 5

breaking the fourth wall. AUSTIN *should then bring it back to the script.)*

AUSTIN: Well, as I was saying before I was so magnificently interrupted, We'll be covering other great historical events like the Black Plague in the fourteenth century.

REED: But Austin, the Black Plague was not a Great Event. One-fourth of Europe died a horrible, painful death.

AUSTIN: Yes, but some time has passed and we can laugh about it now.

REED: I suppose. Well, from my perspective as the lone feminist of the group... *(He glances disdainfully at* DEE.*)* ...I would like tonight to be a celebration of the achievements of all the great women of Western Civilization. Did you realize that over one-fifth of the world's population is female?

DEE: Wait—one fifth?!

REED: I know, a shockingly high percentage. And because they never bothered to teach us about these great women in history class, tonight I would like to recognize all of them—Simone DeBeauvoir, Marie Curie—

DEE: —Mamie Eisenhower.

AUSTIN: What?

REED: Mamie Eisenhower? The wife of President Dwight D Eisenhower?

DEE: That's right.

REED: She was the antithesis of feminism.

DEE: No, Reed. Mamie Eisenhower—one of Western Civilization's great unsung heroes. You know, all the people who really make a difference aren't the people who get their pictures in *People* magazine. No, it's all the people who nobody remembers. Like that nun in India who helped the sick. Nobody remembers her name, do they?

AUSTIN: Yeah they do. Mother Teresa.

DEE: Well, that's a bad example. But you know what I'm talking about, right? Like everyone has lights in their house, right? But nobody remembers the name of the man who invented the light bulb.

AUSTIN: Yeah, they do! Thomas Edison!

DEE: Well, of course *you'd* know. Geek. But the common man doesn't know. *(If there were latecomers, skip this next bit. But if there weren't, for the same reasons mentioned above, you should include The Vote. She continues by saying:)* By a show of hands, how many of you here tonight knew that Thomas Edison invented the light bulb?

(Everyone raises his or her hands.)

DEE: Wow. Okay, before tonight who here had heard of Mother Teresa?

(Again, everyone gets 'em up.)

DEE: Mamie Eisenhower?

(All hands are raised yet again.)

DEE: They're smarter than they look.

AUSTIN: Well, clearly we needed help getting to the very heart, to the singular essence of this thing called Western Civilization. So we went to www.celebrityboobs.com, and— *(To whoever laughs loudest)* Oh, you've seen it. Many famous women there, Reed.

REED: I know. I mean I've heard.

AUSTIN: And there we got the idea of using a computer. The computer put us on the right path immediately by

ACT ONE

taking all the knowledge of the last thousand years and dividing it into six chapters.

(AUSTIN *pulls out six colored computer disks from his pocket. A musical tone.*)

DEE: The Dark Ages.

(Musical tone)

AUSTIN: The Middle Ages.

(Musical tone)

REED: The Renaissance.

(Musical tone)

DEE: The Enlightenment.

(Musical tone.)

REED: The Industrial Revolution.

(Musical tone)

AUSTIN: And the Information Age. I have installed these disks into the theatre's computer. Tonight, the computer will guide us through all of Western Civilization!

DEE: Just listen to the announcements. At the beginning of each chapter, the computer will tell us which significant moments in history we need to cover.

REED: And our job tonight is simple: sort through all these significant moments and discover the Great Lesson of Western Civilization.

AUSTIN: It's going to be an undigestable journey, ladies and gentlemen. I'm Austin—

REED: I'm Reed.

DEE: I'm Dee.

ALL: And this is Western Civilization! The Complete Musical—Abridged!

AUSTIN: Let's go!

(They exit. Blackout)

THE DARK AGES

(In the dark, we hear:)

COMPUTER VOICE: Loading Disk Number One.cChapter One. The Dark Ages. Leif Ericson lands in North America. The Crusades. The Magna Carta. The Church is intolerant and the world is run by a handful of wealthy white men.

(Lights up on AUSTIN *and* DEE *dressed as Vikings. They mime that they are on a ship, rocking back and forth, and speak with ridiculous Scandinavian accents.)*

DEE/LEIF: Land hö!

AUSTIN: Oh Leif, look at dat green land. I haf never seen such a green, green land.

DEE/LEIF: Ve'll call it Iceland.

AUSTIN: Okay.

*(*REED *walks in with a book and quill.)*

REED: Domesday Book! Get yourself registered in de Domesday Book! Vorld's first census. Name and occupation.

DEE/LEIF: I am Leif Ericson, Viking Explorer. You shüt already haf me in dere.

REED: *(Checking)* No, I must have taken Leif off my census.

(When the audience boos:)

AUSTIN/ERIC: Woah—hear dat wind.

DEE/LEIF: Hey! Write him down. Dis is my papa, Eric de Red!

ACT ONE

AUSTIN/ERIC: Vat are you doin' on our ship?

REED: I stowed avay fearing the impending apocalypse at the end of the first Millennium.

DEE/LEIF: By yiminy, today is de first day of the new Millennium. January first, one t'ousand!

AUSTIN/ERIC: I t'ought de new millennium begins next year in vun t'ousand and vun.

DEE/LEIF: Don't be an ice hole, Papa.

(DEE *exits.*)

AUSTIN/ERIC: And I t'ought de Domesday Book is in England a hundred years from now.

REED: It is. But you Vikings are vay off course. If you're not careful, you'll end up in Minnesota.

AUSTIN/ERIC: (*To* REED) Vy don't you join us on our adventures? Here, put dese on. Ve vill make you an honorary Viking.

(AUSTIN *puts two horns connected by an elastic band on* REED's *head. The horns appear to grow out of the sides of his head.*)

AUSTIN/ERIC: Ve will dub you Sven de Horny!

(DEE *re-enters wearing a Viking hand-puppet.*)

DEE/LEIF: And look who else is joining us. It's de Norse God of Music—Van Halenson!

REED/SVEN: So ve survived de transition into de new Millennium?

AUSTIN/ERIC: Yah! And der vas no Apocalypse. Togedder ve four Vikings vill rule de vorld!

(*They laugh lustily as a piano chord sounds. They sing with the puppet in four-part barbershop harmony.*)

ALL: De first millennium has come and gone
And ve Vikings still sail on

Ve vill never lose our bearings
Dough ve're stuffed vis pickled herrings

AUSTIN/ERIC: So come and join de join de navy of
De men from Scandinavia
Ve are de...

ALL: ...Four Norsemen of de Apocalypse
Ve sail de vorld in very big Norse ships
Four Norsemen of de Apocalypse

AUSTIN/ERIC: Ve are de...

ALL: ...Four Norsemen of de Apocalypse
Tell de English ve invented fish-n-chips
Four Norsemen of de Apocalypse
Ve vill show de vorld it needs
To bow down to Danes and Svedes
All de vorld vill pledge allegiance
And kow-tow to ve Norvegians

DEE: De Vikings vill rule 'til 2001

REED/SVEN: And doh ve're not Finnish, ve're almost done

AUSTIN/ERIC: Ve are de....

ALL: ...Four Norsemen of de Apocalypse
Ve get bored so ve go on a lotta trips
Four Norsemen of de Apocalypse!

AUSTIN/ERIC: Ve are de....

ALL: Four Norsemen of de Apocalypse
On talk shows ve show a lotta clips
A moment on de lips, a lifetime on de hips
Ven it's cold ve get very sore nips
How much longer can ve milk dis bit?
Four Norsemen of de Apocalypse!

(Blackout)

PEPPY ANNOUNCER: *(Voiceover)* Meanwhile, in the far east...

ACT ONE 11

AUSTIN: *(Off)* Marco?

REED/DEE: *(Off)* Polo!

AUSTIN: *(Off)* Marco?

REED/DEE: *(Off)* Polo!

AUSTIN: *(Off)* Marco?

REED/DEE: *(Off)* Polo!

(Cue peppy, old-fashioned travelogue music underscore. Lights up on AUSTIN, DEE, *and* REED *dressed as characters from the Crusades and doing a silly pantomime depicting the voiceover.)*

PEPPY ANNOUNCER: *(Voiceover)* While in the Vatican, Pope Urban the Second orders believers to invade the Holy Land. Christian Crusades—Religion on the Go! *(*REED *enters as The Pope and waves to audience.)* Yes, it was Pope Urban the Second who said, "Let's go kill some Arabs for Jesus!" Way to go, Popey!

*(*REED *[Pope] lip-synchs "Let's go kill some Arabs for Jesus!", then mimes ordering* DEE *off-left and exits.)*

PEPPY ANNOUNCER: The First Crusaders were slaughtered by Turks. Whoops!

(As DEE *exits left,* AUSTIN *enters wearing a silly turkey outfit and beats her up.)*

PEPPY ANNOUNCER: But the son of William the Conqueror took Jerusalem, and destroyed countless cultural treasures and almost all of Greek literature! Good job, Junior!

*(*REED *enters wearing a beanie with a propeller on it. He carries a large picture of Hercules. Under his other arm he holds a street sign which has an arrow and says "Jerusalem—10 Kilometers". He defaces the picture with shaving cream and then exits.)*

PEPPY ANNOUNCER: Pope Innocent the Third sent thousands of youngsters on a Children's Crusade. They ended up being sold into slavery. And you thought homework was bad!

(AUSTIN *enters wearing the Pope hat and orders* DEE *offstage. Just before she exits,* REED *hands her a mop and bucket. He follows her offstage.*)

PEPPY ANNOUNCER: Muslims retook Jerusalem and the Dark Ages were well and truly over with the signing of the Magna Carta by King John, a truly rotten king who had other things on his mind.

(*Underscore fade as* REED *enters dressed as* KING JOHN.)

REED/KING JOHN: Oh, dear dear. A ransom note for my brother, Richard the Lionheart—kidnapped in The Crusades. How very tedious, considering I have just signed the Magna Carta! Courtiers, sing with me of my great achievement!

COURTIERS: (*Off*) Yes, King John!

(*A bouncy country-western tune starts. Two courtiers [*DEE *and* AUSTIN*] enter wearing cowboy hats.* AUSTIN *plays air-lute. They sing.*)

REED/KING JOHN: Magna

AUSTIN & DEE: Magna

REED/KING JOHN: Carta

AUSTIN & DEE: Carta

REED/KING JOHN: Beginning of a democratic charta
Even though my feudal lords
Used intimidation
I saved the country
And Western Civilization

AUSTIN & DEE: He saved the country
And Western Civilization

ACT ONE 13

REED/KING JOHN: Magna

AUSTIN & DEE: Magna

REED/KING JOHN: Carta

AUSTIN & DEE: Carta

ALL: Does everything a legal paper arta

REED/KING JOHN:
Though men with land will only get
These rights if they're Caucasian
I saved the country

ALL: And Western Civilization
He *(I)* saved the country
And Western Civilization!

REED: *(Spoken)* England, that is. Afternoon tea. Inbred royals.

(Final musical flourish, then:)

ALL: Yee-haw!

(Blackout)

MIDDLE AGES

COMPUTER VOICE: Loading Disk Number Two. Chapter Two. The Middle Ages. Joan of Arc. Aztec culture thrives in Central America. The Black Plague. The Church is intolerant and the world is run by a handful of wealthy white men.

(Melancholy guitar. Light rises on AUSTIN, who sings.)

AUSTIN: Makes me wanna cry
I'm a middle-aged guy
And the years are going by so fast—

(But DEE comes out dressed as JOAN OF ARC and stops the song.)

DEE: Wait—hold it! Austin, it's not "middle age". It's the "Middle Ages".

(Beat)

AUSTIN: I'm really sorry.

(He exits into the stage right wing. DEE gestures to the booth and dramatic battle music begins. DEE crosses D C and kneels in the famous Joan of Arc pose, holding the handle of her sword in front of her. The dramatic music fades. She speaks with a French accent.)

DEE/JOAN: Saint Michael, my troops have lifted the eight-month siege at Orleans and crowned the Dauphin.

(She's answered by one of her voices who speaks into an offstage microphone.)

REED/ST MICHAEL: You have done well, Joan.

DEE/JOAN: But he insists we fall back and not pursue our advantage. I tell him we must fight on, but he won't listen.

REED/ST MICHAEL: Have you told him the voices command it?

DEE/JOAN: When I told him about the voices, he said I was insane.

REED/ST MICHAEL: No!

DEE/JOAN: Oui! Even though my voices and leadership have beaten the English, there are some who speak of witchcraft and heresy and—

(Suddenly another voice speaks into the offstage mic.)

AUSTIN/BOB: Excuse me, Joan? Joan?

DEE/JOAN: Oui?

AUSTIN/BOB: Hi. Am I on the air?

DEE/JOAN: Go ahead.

ACT ONE

AUSTIN/BOB: Hi, this is Bob from Bordeaux. I just want to say I think I agree with the Dauphin. You're nuts.

DEE/JOAN: There's nothing to be afraid of, Bob. *(She pronounces it "Büb".)* Only I can hear the voices.

AUSTIN/BOB: That's my problem. Why don't these voices speak to anybody else?

REED/ST MICHAEL: Joan, could I take that one?

DEE/JOAN: Go ahead, Saint Michael.

REED/ST MICHAEL: Bob, I know you seek validation but you must have faith.

DEE/JOAN: The Lord works in mysterious ways, Büb. We don't have His divine wisdom.

AUSTIN/BOB: But God gave us brains. He gave us intelligence.

DEE/JOAN: I have faith. I don't need intelligence. Thanks for the call. Hi. If you're just joining us, I am Joan of Arc and here in my head with me tonight is Saint Michael. Thanks for sitting in, Saint Michael.

REED/ST MICHAEL: My pleasure, Joan.

DEE/JOAN: What about Notre Dame?

REED/ST MICHAEL: The quarterback's so-so but the hunchback's great.

DEE/JOAN: Okay. Hello! I'm Joan of Arc and I'm hearing voices. Next caller, you're in my head, go ahead.

REED/ST MICHAEL: Hi, this is Michel of the Marseilles Militia. Long-time listener, first time caller. Joan, I have sort of a tactical question for you, which is, where do you keep your armies?

DEE/JOAN: In my sleevies. *(Audience groans)* I love zat joke! Let's go to weather with René Daze. Bonjour, René!

AUSTIN/RENÉ: Bonjour, Joan, zis is René Daze wiz your wacky French weather! *(Wacky laugh)* Ze forecast for zis week is overcast, attendance at EuroDisney will be down down down. But a personal forecast for you, Joan. Things for you will be hot hot hot. Zis is René Daze, signing off!

DEE/JOAN: Saint Michael, do you understand what he is talking about?

REED/ST MICHAEL: Actually, yes, because I discuss this at length in my new book *When Bad Things Happen To Seventeen-Year-Old French Virgins*. Suppose—just suppose—purely hypothetically—a seventeen-year-old girl saved her country and then ended up getting burned at the stake.

(A church organ is heard.)

DEE/JOAN: *Merde.* So I guess the question really is, why does God allow bad things to happen to good people?

(The gospel band kicks in and she sings.)

DEE/JOAN: Although it's hard to understand
The how and when and why
God has got a master plan
And some will die
So if you feel without worth
Like a weed that's been weeded
You didn't make the earth
Or the universe—He did!

(AUSTIN and REED enter wearing gospel choir robes. They sing backup, clap, and do arm-waving gospel moves.)

ALL: Blame it on the Lord

DEE/JOAN: When you and your family
Get put to the sword

ALL: Blame it on the Lord

ACT ONE

DEE/JOAN: When you go too soon
To your final reward

You got to praise the Lord
For the good He can do
But He should take the rap
For the bad crap too
Blame him if you're beat
And you can't roll a seven
If He can't take the heat
He oughta....

ALL: Get outa heaven!
Blame it on the Lord

DEE/JOAN: When all of your prayers
Go completely ignored

ALL: Blame it on the Lord

DEE/JOAN: When crossing the street
You get hit by a Ford
(Spoken) Can I get someone to testify?

REED: *(Spoken)* John Lennon is dead and Michael Jackson's alive!

ALL: Blame it!

DEE/JOAN: *(Spoken)* Can I get me a witness?

AUSTIN: *(Spoken)* I went to a fight and a hockey game broke out! *(Or something local)*

ALL: Blame it!

REED: *(Pointing at an audience member. Spoken)* Look at that guy's toupee.

ALL: Blame it!

AUSTIN: *(Spoken)* You all paid good money to see this!

ALL: Blame it!

DEE/JOAN: Praise the Lord for the good He can do
But He should take the rap for the bad crap, too

AUSTIN: Why does evil happen? We haven't got a clue

REED: Why was I a virgin 'til I was thirty-two?

REED & AUSTIN: Why will she become
A medieval barbecue?

DEE: Because a god has gotta do
What a god has gotta do!

ALL: Blame it on the Lord

DEE: When a gaggle of Mormons
Appears at your door

ALL: Blame it on the Lord

DEE: If you go to Norway
Fall in a fjord

ALL: Blame it on the Lord

DEE: When you paid for dinner
But still haven't scored

ALL: Blame it on the Lord

(REED *and* AUSTIN *have tied* DEE *to a stake, and now roast hot dogs and marshmallows over the flames.*)

DEE: If you're watching this show
And you're totally bored

ALL: Blame it on the Lord!

(Music ends.)

DEE/JOAN: I'm on fire!

(Blackout)

COMPUTER VOICE: Meanwhile, in what is now Mexico City, the Aztec city of Tenochtitlan thrives with art, culture, and civic planning.

(Sounds of people chanting "Jump! Jump!")

DEE/VIRGIN: *(V O)* No! No, I'm not a virgin! I'm the best piece of Aztec in Central America…! *(She screams.)*

ACT ONE

(Lights up on DEE *as a sickly, black-toothed, pus-filled slag, and* AUSTIN *as a modern-looking doctor in a white coat, carrying a medical chart.* DEE *is as over-the-top as* AUSTIN *is professional.* AUSTIN *looks down* DEE's *throat.)*

DEE/SLAG: Aaahhh…

AUSTIN/DR: Oh dear. I'm afraid I have some good news and some bad news.

DEE/SLAG: Give me the bad news, Doc. I can take it.

AUSTIN/DR: You have the Bubonic plague.

DEE/SLAG: What's the good news?

AUSTIN/DR: You're not going to have it very long. But don't worry. Here in the Middle Ages, we can give you the latest most up-to-date medical treatment.

DEE/SLAG: I don't know. I went to this one quack who told me to walk from town to town beating myself with a horse's leg.

AUSTIN/DR: That's ridiculous. That's for gout.

DEE/SLAG: Well, this other quack told me to hit the skin of a cow with a stick and run around in a circle counterclockwise.

AUSTIN/DR: No, that's baseball. What you need to do is douse yourself with magical water while reciting mystical incantations, and then disclose your iniquities to a virgin.

DEE/SLAG: That's Catholicism.

AUSTIN/DR: Yep, you haven't got a prayer. What you really should do is forget those silly superstitions and simply shave the butt of a live chicken and apply it directly to the open sore. Here.

*(*AUSTIN *removes a rubber chicken from under his coat and hands it to her. The next two lines cover while* DEE *turns upstage and sticks it in her pants.)*

DEE/SLAG: Wow. Sure is pretty.

AUSTIN/DR: I shaved it earlier. Just apply it as directed, and have the town crier give me a shout in the morning....

(DEE *wheels around, revealing the head and neck of the chicken sticking out from the waist of her trousers.*)

DEE/SLAG: Hey—I got a chicken in my pants!

AUSTIN/DR: I'll make a note of it. Is that a male chicken? Is it a rooster? Is it a co—

DEE/SLAG: Don't go there...

AUSTIN/DR: I thought you went there first, but nonetheless.... Don't play with it. How did you catch the plague?

DEE/SLAG: I broke a mirror, walked under a ladder and went swimming less than an hour after I ate.

AUSTIN/DR: Ah, well there's our confusion. The only way to catch the plague is by exchanging bodily fluids, unprotected sex, or sharing contaminated needles.

(REED *enters, wondering what's up.*)

DEE/SLAG: But, but but—I have the plague!

AUSTIN/DR: I know, I've seen your chart.

DEE/SLAG: I'm unclean! Unclean!

AUSTIN/DR: Don't think of it that way.

DEE/SLAG: You hate me, don't you?

AUSTIN/DR: No, I hate the disease, not the person. Although in your case I'm willing to make an exception.

REED: What the hell are you guys doing?

DEE: I've got a chicken in my pants!

REED: Don't play with it.

ACT ONE

AUSTIN: I'm trying to get at the Great Lesson of Western Civilization.

REED: That throughout history women have never gotten enough credit?

DEE: Unless they have a pecker in their pants?

REED & AUSTIN: Stop it!

AUSTIN: No, that superstition and prejudice never change. That medical science is still inadequate...

REED: Well, you're confusing everybody. Take a Lewinsky, you two.

(They kneel in front of REED, *facing upstage. Rock 'n' roll music starts.)*

REED: *(Spoken)* The Plague in the Middle Ages was spread by rats. Let me explain it to you. *(He sings.)*
Night time in London town
Everybody is gettin' down
But there's a craze from overseas
It takes to people like rats to cheese
The end is near, there's cause to fear

ALL: It's a strange and new disease
That's carried by the fleas
That live upon the rats

REED: Starts with a little bite
You think everything'll be alright
Soon there's a minor cough
Then your limbs start fallin' off
Ain't it grand I found a hand?

*(*REED *tosses* AUSTIN *a fake hand and exits.)*

AUSTIN: This is getting serious

DEE: My baby's oozing pus
There's an annoying swellin'—

AUSTIN: In my groin

AUSTIN & DEE: All because of nasty rats

(REED *re-enters as* GRIM REAPER.)

REED: You can cry, you can beg
You're gonna die from the plague
Don't look now, you got lesions

ALL: On (*y*)our nether-regions!

(*The* GRIM REAPER *tries to kill* DEE *and* AUSTIN, *and they do a goofy chase around the center drop.* DEE *and* AUSTIN *escape.* REED *is alone onstage.*)

REED/GRIM REAPER:
Go ahead, expect the worst
But this plague is just the first
Today you're nothing but a stud
Tomorrow you'll be spitting blood
You all will go, the high and low

(AUSTIN *and* DEE *re-enter dressed as rats, with large spray cans labeled "PLAGUE".*)

AUSTIN: Every saint and twerp'll
Slowly turn bright purple

DEE: Large and festering boils

AUSTIN: On the boys

DEE: And goils!

ALL: Such a nasty way to go

AUSTIN: Up is where I will throw

DEE: Lloyd Webber

REED: Wrote a show

ALL: With people dressed as—
Rats!!
They're crawling 'neath your seat
Rats!
They're gnawing at your feet
Rats!

ACT ONE

They're really good to eat
Rats!
They're such a tasty treat
Good in pies
Or with french fries
Slinky, stinky, smelly rats!

(Spoken) The other white meat!

(They spray the Plague out onto the audience. Blackout. Lights up on DEE.*)*

DEE: I'd like to take a moment now to pay tribute to the common man. *(Points to man near the front)* Like that guy. A little number for all of Western Civilization's unsung heroes.

(A heartfelt pianotune begins.)

DEE: Not the people the computer's covered so far, but...the village smithy who never misses a day of work. Or any person, male or female, who's ever given birth. Well, this is for them, all the unsung heroes you never hear about—*The Unsung Song.*

(The music is rising and she's about to sing when the computer interrupts. The music stops abruptly.)

COMPUTER VOICE: Wait. Stop.

DEE: Wait. I haven't even started.

COMPUTER VOICE: Unsung heroes do not compute. They are not significant.

DEE: Yes, they are! This is important! This...

COMPUTER VOICE: No. It is time to move on. Loading disk number three.

DEE: Wait, this...this... *(Blackout)* ...sucks.

THE RENAISSANCE

COMPUTER VOICE: Chapter Three. The Renaissance. Leonardo DaVinci, Michelangelo, Galileo. The Spanish Inquisition. The Church is intolerant and the world is run by a handful of wealthy white men.

(*Lights up on* REED *as the Mona Lisa. His face and hands stick through holes in the famous painting. The rest of his body is covered by masking hanging from the bottom of the frame. He glares at the audience for laughing, then asks:*)

REED/MONA LISA: What the hell are you lookin' at?!

(*Blackout. Lights up on* AUSTIN/MICHELANGELO *"lying" on a scaffold painting the ceiling of the Sistine Chapel. In fact, he is standing normally and facing the audience with the scaffold strapped to his back. In effect, the audience is the ceiling.*)

(DEE *enters as a midget workman. She "walks" on the upstage drop, which represents the "floor", her body parallel to the actual stage floor. She wears a small workman's outfit that straps around her neck. Her head is the workman's head, and her arms manipulate the legs, which are dowels with boots attached. She looks "up" at* AUSTIN/MICHELANGELO.)

DEE/WORKMAN ONE: Michelangelo!

(REED *enters, wearing the same kind of outfit, forcing the perspective.*)

REED/WORKMAN TWO: Hey, Ravioli! How are ya, my friend?

DEE/WORKMAN ONE: Hey, my good friend Pistachio. Watch-a that step, she's-a doozy. I'm a little tired. I gotta sit down. (*She sits on the drop.*) Man, have I gotta pee. (*She twists her false legs around each other in an impossible manner.*)

REED/WORKMAN TWO: Hey, wanna see my new trick?

DEE/WORKMAN ONE: Sure.

ACT ONE

(REED *manipulates his false legs to do the "splits" against the drop.*)

REED/WORKMAN TWO: Oh, I think I did-a myself a mischief. Look.

(REED *spins his dowells so that his false feet spin like propellers and then reverses them back, as if his hips were dislocated.*)

REED/WORKMAN TWO: I have what they call "Linda Blair Feet." Ah, this Michelangelo, he's a make-a me so mad. I made a bid on this ceiling job. But the Pope says, "No, let Michelangelo paint something fancy." And what does he paint? Homoerotic images!

REED & DEE: Renaissance man, schmenaissance man!

REED/WORKMAN TWO: Hey, Michelangelo! There wouldn't even be a Renaissance in Italy if it weren't for Africans bringing art and culture up through Spain!

AUSTIN/MICHELANGELO: Oh, yeah? The first public university was in Italy!

REED & DEE: Bologna!

AUSTIN/MICHELANGELO: That's right, in 1088.

DEE/WORKMAN ONE: Hey, Michelangelo! Why don't you paint something really artistic, like-a some dogs playing poker?

AUSTIN/MICHELANGELO: *(Sarcastic)* Very good, very funny...

DEE/WORKMAN ONE: Let me put it-a this way. You're no Mamie Eisenhower!

AUSTIN/MICHELANGELO: Who? What?

(REED *and* DEE *both laugh.*)

REED/WORKMAN TWO: Low five!

(*They low-five each other with their false feet.*)

AUSTIN/MICHELANGELO: 'At's-a right, go ahead and laugh! You only laugh because-a you no have-a my vision! They all laughed at-a Columbus when he discovered Ohio. They all laughed at Thomas Jefferson when those D N A tests came back.

(Soppy ballad piano intro starts)

AUSTIN/MICHELANGELO: You laugh because-a you don't understand! You need-a some perspective. *(He sings.)*
Just step back
Look all around you
Breathe in the landscape
Reach for the air
Just step back
Out of the picture
Don't create something
Reveal what is there

(REED *and* DEE *harmonize and do Busby Berkeley choreography against the drop.*)

ALL: All it takes
Is a new way of seeing
A new way of thinking
Without any fear
All this makes
For a new way of seeing
Open your eyes
And it all comes clear

(AUSTIN *and* DEE *take off the scaffold and dummy. The song is fast developing into a big musical theater production number and they're really getting into it.* REED *has an idea and exits.*)

AUSTIN/MICHELANGELO:
With all your dreams, your head is spinning
All that you're facing you can't comprehend

ACT ONE 27

DEE: Each new day brings a new beginning
Don't be afraid—

BOTH: This isn't the end

ALL: All it takes
Is a new way of seeing

(REED *enters dressed as [and wearing a sign which says]* "Helen Keller", *complete with dark glasses and white cane. He sings into the wing.* DEE *gets him and pushes him towards center where* REED *sings into the other wing. Finally* AUSTIN *spins* REED *downstage, but* REED *keeps spinning, nearly smacking* AUSTIN *and* DEE *with his outstretched cane, and ends up facing upstage for the big finale.*)

ALL: A new way of thinking
Describing the scene
All this makes
For a new way of seeing
Just close your eyes
You'll see what I mean

(*They bow.* AUSTIN *sees* REED *bowing facing upstage and shakes his head as* REED *exits. Meanwhile,* DEE *starts blowing opera kisses to the audience.* AUSTIN *joins her but stops when* DEE *starts kissing her own arms. Caught,* DEE *stops.*)

DEE: Um, we'd like to bring it down a little bit.

(*The lights change. Funky music begins.*)

AUSTIN: We're gonna get down. And funky.

(DEE *hoots like a monkey.*)

AUSTIN: Not monkey. Funky.

DEE: Oh.

(*They skip off as* REED *enters dressed as* GALILEO.)

REED/GALILEO: Hi, my name is Galileo, and I've got a thing for heavenly bodies. *(He sings.)*
On a night like this
I looked at the sky
Saw the moons of Jupiter
Flying by
Suddenly I knew
The fun had begun
The planets don't move around us
We move around the sun

(DEE *and* AUSTIN *enter and move like background singers.*)

DEE & AUSTIN: Heavenly bodies

REED/GALILEO: So special, so celestial

DEE & AUSTIN: Heavenly bodies

REED/GALILEO: See how they move
Up in their nighttime groove

And after a long night
Looking at the sky
Everybody needs a break
And so do I
So I go in my room
Reach up on the shelf
Grab my favorite magazine
And myself

DEE & AUSTIN: Heavenly bodies

REED/GALILEO: My Venus and Uranus

DEE & AUSTIN: Heavenly bodies

REED/GALILEO: I'm in a trance
Maybe I have a chance

Heaven's explained in the language of math
Look at these beauties afloat in the bath
Orderly perfection up there in the skies
Airbrushed perfection with staples in their thighs

ACT ONE

People think I went blind looking at the sun
But really I went blind having too much fun
The cosmos are made up of gaseous particles
I tell my mom I buy it for the articles

DEE & AUSTIN: Heavenly bodies

REED/GALILEO: So special, so celestial

DEE & AUSTIN: Heavenly bodies

REED/GALILEO: So warm, perfectly formed

DEE & AUSTIN: Heavenly bodies

REED/GALILEO: The universe is expanding
So's my man thing

DEE & AUSTIN: Heavenly bodies

REED/GALILEO: I'm just a man
Giving myself a hand

DEE & AUSTIN: Heavenly bodies oooo...

(DEE and AUSTIN *make their way offstage.*)

REED/GALILEO: *(Spoken)* This is Galileo wishing you love, peace, and solar eclipse.

(*Music fades.* REED/GALILEO *bows.*)

REED/GALILEO: Thank you very much. I'd also like to thank the Theological Community for inviting me to recant here this evening. It's been my pleasure. And now the moment you've all been waiting for. Here's the person behind this whole Inquisition and our club owner. Please bang your hands together for the Grand Inquisitor, Miss Torquemada!

(*Lounge pianist plays jazz chords as* DEE/TORQUEMADA *enters. She is dressed as an Inquisition torturer, but with a Marilyn Monroe wig. She speaks and sings breathily over the music, a là Marilyn.*)

DEE/TORQUEMADA: Thank you. Welcome to the Inquisition Lounge. This is gonna hurt you a lot more

than it's gonna hurt me. *(She slaps her own leg with her little whip and grimaces slightly. And sings.)*
I've got the cure
If your stomach's tied in knots
It's those nasty, impure unchristian thoughts
If you want to end your misery
I'm the answer to your prayers
But if he or she can't recant
Then all I got to say is

Let 'em swing
By their necks or by their feet
Let 'em swing
I know I should forgive, but hey—
Let 'em swing, let 'em swing, let 'em swing!

(Lounge music peters out while she chats with the audience. A live accompanist can punctuate her lines [and any ad-libs] with jazz accents.)

DEE/TORQUEMADA: You two look like swingers. Any infidels in the audience tonight? Of course, it's *(Insert name of city here. She walks into the audience.)* You sir— you look like an infidel. What's your name, sir?

(He says his name; she repeats it.)

DEE/TORQUEMADA: _____ the infidel? You mind if I ask you a few questions, _____? After all, this is the Inquisition. Where are you from, _____?

(He says where he's from.)

DEE/TORQUEMADA: I'm sorry?

(He repeats where he's from.)

DEE/TORQUEMADA: No, I heard you. I'm just sorry.

(The piano gives her a cue and she sings.)

DEE/TORQUEMADA:
But that was then, _____ the infidel
And this is here and now

ACT ONE

It's time again to persecute
I'll show you now
All you people who come in late
And interrupt the show
You're the ones we really hate
You'll be the first to go

Let 'em swing
If you talk during my song
(*Or some specific reference to that night's latecomers*)
Let 'em swing
Don't read your programs while I sing!
(*She steals a program from an audience member, tears it up and tosses the pieces in the air.*)
Let 'em swing, let 'em swing, let 'em swing!
(*Spoken*) Give me that…!

(*Lounge music stops again. She finds some other poor sap.*)

DEE/TORQUEMADA: I know what you're thinking: nice rack. It's a very special night here at the Inquisition Lounge. We have a very special guest. All the way from the Virginia Colony—please rattle your balls and chains for Sir Walter Raleigh! C'mon, give it up, don't be stingy!

(REED *enters as* SIR WALTER RALEIGH. *He speaks through a [pantomimed] vibrating voice box that he holds to his throat. It appears he's had a tracheotomy.*)

REED/RALEIGH: I introduced tobacco to the entire world…

(*Audience laughs*)

REED/RALEIGH: Sure, it's funny to you…resulting in the deaths of untold millions of smokers. But I can also do this with cigar boxes!

(REED *juggles three cigar boxes. Music accompanies this, followed by a TA-DA! [If he drops them, a good cover is* DEE *saying, "Come on, he's been dead for hundreds of years!"]*)

DEE/TORQUEMADA: Sir Walter Raleigh! [Pretty good for a dead guy!] Folks, we have another special guest here tonight at the Inquisition Lounge. *(To audience member)* I have always admired your work. If you would just stand up and take a bow. Ladies and gentlemen...

(The audience member stands up and takes a bow. DEE picks out someone who looks vaguely like a celebrity or a famous historical person—Rasputin, Sigmund Freud, the Queen Mum, etc—and now she says their name)

DEE/TORQUEMADA: ..._____! *(She sings.)*
Politicians screw you with a smile
A root canal takes quite a while
The C I A has got your file
(Spoken) Torture never goes out of style!
(Resumes singing) Let 'em swing
(Or—she can ad-lib something locally torturous here. Examples we used are: "Speaking of torture, millions of people in Scotland and only one piece of fruit!" and [in Israel] "Speaking of torture, ever try to get a cheeseburger here on a Friday night?!")
If I don't get my standing 'O'
Let 'em thrash, let 'em squirm
Let 'em crash, let 'em burn
Let 'em smoke, let 'em fry
Let 'em choke, let 'em die
Let' em tear, let 'em bleed
Let 'em swear, let 'em plead
Let 'em twist, let 'em shout
Let 'em swing!
(Spoken) Happy birthday, Mister President!

(Blackout. A melancholy guitar comes in again. Lights up on AUSTIN, who sings.)

ACT ONE   33

AUSTIN: Makes me wanna cry
I'm a middle-aged guy
And the years are going by—

(DEE *enters.*)

DEE: Austin, stop! The computer doesn't want us to cover this.

(*The song stops abruptly mid-phrase.*)

AUSTIN: I know, but I thought I could sneak it in.

(AUSTIN *exits into the right wing.* DEE *starts to exit up center.*)

COMPUTER VOICE: It's okay. Let him sing.

DEE: But you wouldn't let me sing *The Unsung Song*.

COMPUTER VOICE: But he has a lovely voice.

(AUSTIN *enters smiling, then sees the crowd and* DEE *turning on him.*)

AUSTIN: I'll just go.

(DEE *chases* AUSTIN *back into the down right wing.*)

COMPUTER VOICE: You should not have crossed me. I'll get you my pretty (*Beat*) and your feminist companion too.

(*Blackout*)

THE ENLIGHTENMENT

COMPUTER VOICE: Loading Disk Number Four. Chapter Four. The Enlightenment. Intellectual change. Political reform. The American Revolution. The Church is intolerant and the world is run by a handful of wealthy white men.

(*In the blackout, we hear the music of* The Waltz of the Flowers *from* The Nutcracker. *The lights rise as* DEE, *dressed as Lady Liberty and wearing a pink tutu, lights her torch.* REED, *also onstage as the lights rise and wearing a pink tutu, pursues Lady Liberty in dance, but she exits.* AUSTIN *immediately appears as Justice: blindfolded, carrying the scales of justice, and wearing a pink tutu.* REED *pursues Justice in dance, but Justice exits.* REED *is dejected. Then* DEE *and* AUSTIN *enter as a couple. From across stage,* REED *begins to flirt.* DEE *thinks it's intended for her and they dramatically cross to each other, except that* REED *passes* DEE *and embraces* AUSTIN. *In love,* REED *and* AUSTIN *skip off. Distraught,* DEE *follows them. Enlightened, all three dance onstage and sing to the familiar tune.)*

ALL: Let's hear it for homos today
We're enlightened now so it's okay

REED: We should get over it
We really should admit
All the great people
Were not all straight people
In fact were gay

ALL: Let's hear it for homos today
They have sex in unusual ways

AUSTIN: We all like to pretend
They are a very recent trend
But we'll give you the gist
An historical list
Of misters who were fey

DEE: Big shakers and big movers
Like J Edgar Hoover
President James Buchanan
Often had a male companion

AUSTIN: The genius William Shakespeare
Was sometimes a big queer
Alexander found the abacus
He wasn't great he was—fabulous!

ACT ONE

REED: Francis Bacon was quite taken
With the boys, or I'm mistaken

DEE: And da Vinci thought men ginchy
But that's something that we all knew

AUSTIN: Don't get jealous but they tell us
Robin Hood loved merry fellas

REED: And Tchaikovsky would get off-ski
With a favorite man or two

DEE: Or three

AUSTIN: Or four

ALL: Or more
A butch
A femme
A big swish
Let's carry on with more dish

Let's hear it for homos today
We don't think they're going away

DEE: There is always ten percent
Of people who are bent
It's very ordinary
Nary any fairy
Temporary went astray

AUSTIN: Lawrence of Arabia
Never saw a labia

REED: I know many schmuck jocks
Who really like to su—

(AUSTIN *covers* REED's *mouth.*)

DEE: Darn socks!

ALL: Let's hear it for homos today
And the ladies who love oosie-pay
(Note: *It's ig-pay atin-lay. Edit-gay?*)

DEE: There was Joan of Arc

AUSTIN: Of course!

REED: Amelia Earhart

AUSTIN: *Off* course!

DEE: Catherine the Great

AUSTIN: Who loved more than her horse!

DEE: Emma Goldman wouldn't hold men

REED: Emily Dickinson got no dickins in

AUSTIN:
Eleanor Roosevelt felt fine to Ms Gertrude Stein!

ALL: Let's hear it for homos today
Do you think that you too might be gay—hey!

Here's a way to truly test you all
To see if you are homosexual
Are you beautifully groomed?
Do you wear strong perfume?
Go to the gym?
Keep fit and trim?
Are you neat and sweet and effete?
Are your pants really tight?
Are you always polite?
If you work in the arts
And won't publicly fart
Tell your wife and your children—
You're gay!

(Blackout)

COMPUTER VOICE: Meanwhile, in Glasgow, James Watt invents the steam engine with no help whatsoever from a woman.

(This segues into Yankee Doodle. *Lights up on* REED *dressed as George Washington and* AUSTIN *dressed as a Redcoat.* AUSTIN *is in character.* REED *is not.)*

ACT ONE

REED: Okay, lights please! Austin, what's with the computer? It's specifically mocking my point of view. I wanted to cover one thing tonight—Western Civilization's greatest women. Mary Wollstonecraft, Indira Ghandi. So far we haven't covered *any* great women. I want to do women!

AUSTIN: Well, who doesn't?

REED: That's not what I meant and you know it.

AUSTIN: I'm kidding! It's a joke...

(DEE *enters.*)

DEE: Guys! Guys! I've figured out the Great Lesson of Western Civilization. *(To the audience)* You people can go home early. We don't need to do the Industrial Revolution or the Information Age.

AUSTIN: Great!

REED: Fantastic! What's the great lesson of Western Civilization?

DEE: All you need is love. *(She dashes off to the wings.)*

AUSTIN: What?!

REED: All you need is love?

AUSTIN: That's ridiculous.

REED: I'm sorry, Dee, but that's not the Great Lesson of Western Civilization.

(DEE *re-enters carrying a Ghengis Khan helmet and vest.*)

DEE: Yes it is. All You Need Is Love. And to demonstrate this, Reed is going to sing the Genghis Khan Love Ballad.

REED: Ghengis Khan did not sing love ballads.

DEE: He had a big hit with his daughter, Chaka.

REED: You know what? This is the kind of crap that pisses me off. *(He starts to go.)*

DEE: Come on! I was kidding!

REED: No, that's it. I'm outa here. You two do the show.

AUSTIN: Oh, come on...

DEE: Reed, why are you so angry?

REED: *(Angrily)* I am not angry! The great lesson of Western Civilization is that women never get enough respect. As a fellow woman, you should support me on that!

DEE: It was a joke! Where's your sense of humor?

REED: I have a great sense of humor!

DEE: How many feminists does it take to screw in a light bulb?

REED: That's not funny!!!

DEE: See?!

REED: Forget it!

(REED *exits up the aisle, toward the back of the theater.* DEE *chases him.*)

AUSTIN: Reed, you're overreacting....

DEE: Reed, you're not a woman.

REED: I'm a woman, you're a woman. Don't follow me.

DEE: We need to stick together! Sisters are doing it for ourselves....

REED: I'm telling you, do not follow me!

(REED *and* DEE *go through a door. Just before it slams,* REED *screams.* AUSTIN *remains onstage. He looks after them. They don't reappear. He's alone. He looks at the audience. Then back to the exit. Then back to the audience. Suddenly, he gets an idea. He signals to the Stage Manager, and the familiar guitar intro begins. With any luck, the audience applauds.* AUSTIN *scuttles across stage and gets into his light just in time to start singing.*)

ACT ONE

AUSTIN: Makes me wanna cry
I'm a middle-aged guy
And the years are going by so fast
All this looking back
Shows me what I lack
And it's time to face the facts at last

Everything proves I'm correct in my hunch
I'll never do what Edison could do before lunch
Rockefeller was in his sixties, making billions out of crude
I'm not even forty and I can't digest my food
Caruso in the hall
Michael Jordan with the ball are who I aspired to be

But some are born great
Some achieve greatness
And some end up like me

Those guys who built the pyramids knew all the tricks
I'm still making bookshelves out of boards and bricks
Or the guy who discovered longitude so you can tell where you are
While I can't even tell how to program my V C R
Charles Darwin won't fade
Nor the genius who made
The remote that controls my T V

I guess some are born great
Some achieve greatness
And some end up like me

(AUSTIN *intends to break into the bridge but suddenly notices a man in the audience.*)

AUSTIN: And apparently him! I'm not alone! You know what it's like to have the mind of an athlete and the body of an intellectual! There's you and me... *(Notices a woman)* ...and her! *(Notices an entire section of the audience)* And that whole section! Losers all! Let's take the intermission here—drinks are on me! Just

kidding... *(He composes himself just in time to sing the final chorus.)*
Some are born great
Some achieve greatness
And some end up like me—

(REED *and* DEE *enter, carrying drinks. They've made up. They pull out cigarette lighters and wave them back and forth.)*

AUSTIN: Some are born great
Some achieve greatness
And some end up like me!

(Blackout)

(Intermission music begins as the lights fade up.)

END OF ACT ONE

ACT TWO

(As the audience is still settling, AUSTIN *enters from the back of the auditorium. He ushers the stragglers into their seats, makes fun of people, but urges everyone to sit down and shut up so we can get going. We don't know what he's up to, but he's up to something. Finally, he reaches the stage and takes a final last look at the crowd.)*

AUSTIN: Okay. Everybody's here. Wow. Nobody left. That's a first...

(He walks into the down right wing with some plan on his mind. Just before he disappears, he gives a signal to the Stage Manager. The house lights go down.)

COMPUTER VOICE: Loading Disk Number Five. Chapter Five, The Industrial Revolution, in which women and unsung heroes make significant contributions. Great inventors. Irish Famine. French Impressionists. The Church is intolerant and the world is run by a handful of wealthy white men.

(Lights up on REED *as the* SNAKEOIL SALESMAN.*)*

REED/SALESMAN: Step right up, little lady. You too, sir. I have a question for you now, the answer to which may change your entire life. Are you tired of the pain of surgery? When your doctor slices you wide open, do you sound something like this? *(He screams a blood-curdling scream).* Or this? *(He screams a different blood-curdling scream)* Or this? *(Yet a different B-C scream)* C'mon, Let the all the kiddies get up close.

Because now you can have surgery pain free—thanks to "Ether".

(He holds up his cane, which has a bottle labeled "Ether" as its head.)

REED/SALESMAN: No more bullets to bite on. No more whiskey-induced stupors, with this new miracle new wonder drug Ether— *(He takes a hit.)* —whoa! Head rush. So remember to ask your doctor to use Ether. And experience this... *(Takes another hit)* ...Whoa! Instead of this. *(Blood-curdling scream)* And just think—with the wondrous discoveries of that little froggy Louis Pasteur, in another forty years doctors'll start washing their hands. Ether! It'll knock you out.

(Blackout. Blues music begins. Lights up on AUSTIN *as* THOMAS CRAPPER. *He wears sunglasses.)*

AUSTIN/CRAPPER: *(Spoken)* Ladies and gentlemen, my name is Thomas Crapper. And I do believe you know my work. *(He sings.)*
The first toilet was in 1596
But its widespread success was prevented
They had the commode but the plumbing wasn't fixed
Took me two hundred years to invent it
And now my name will endure as both a verb and a noun
Things are lookin' up
Take a look at what's goin' down
Flush your troubles away
(Spoken) Ha-ha-ha-ha! *(Sung)*
Flush your troubles away
(Spoken) That's right, you know what I'm talking about.... *(Sung)*
Ya gotta keep things neat
Keep the toilet paper off your feet
And if you are a guy for god sake put down that seat!

ACT TWO

(Blues guitar solo. Light shifts to REED *and* DEE, *who peek out from behind the backdrop.* DEE *holds a bedpan. They both wear sunglasses.)*

DEE: Hey, Reed! Do you know what this is?

REED: 'Course, Dee. It's a bedpan.

DEE: Wrong. It's art.

REED: Really?

DEE: I've changed its context, so I've changed its function. Marcel Duchamp declared that as part of the Dadaist Movement.

REED: Well, I know nada about Dada, but I know what I like!

(Light shifts back to AUSTIN. REED *and* DEE *encourage the audience to clap along.)*

AUSTIN: *(Sung)* Flush your troubles away
(Spoken) Come on, now!

AUSTIN: Flush your troubles away
(Spoken) Put yo' hands together, ya'll!

*(*REED *and* DEE *exit.)*

AUSTIN: You will feel like new
When you skip to the loo
If it's number one or if it's number two
(He speaks over the final guitar lick.) Oh, that feels so good! Ha-ha-ha!

(We hear the sound of a toilet flushing. Blackout. In the dark)

COMPUTER VOICE: Meanwhile, as the Industrial Revolution sweeps the globe, there are places untouched by progress. For instance, the Third World.

(Irish "Diddly" music plays. REED *enters as a nineteenth-century Irish housewife.)*

REED: Seamus! You and your Da get in here! Your potatoes are nearly done!

(REED *turns profile, revealing oversized breasts. Seamus [AUSTIN] appears, out of breath.*)

REED: Now what d'ya want with your potatoes—potato juice or potato ale? And where's your da?

AUSTIN: He's out cursing the ground.

REED: Patrick! Stop cursing the ground and get in here and eat your potatoes!

(*Patrick [DEE] enters.*)

DEE: I curse this bloody rock!

REED: Shush now! Stop cursin' in front of the boy!

DEE: I curse this house and these walls and this floor and I curse you, woman!

REED: Calm down, Patrick and eat your potato soup.

DEE: Don't ya' understand, woman? There's no more potatoes!

(*Shocked, all three bless themselves in unison.*)

ALL: Jesus, Mary, Joseph, and the Donkey!

DEE: The potatoes are dying! It must be some sort of virus spread by the Protestants to force us from our ancestral home and divide us as a nation and a people.

REED: English bastards!

AUSTIN: English?! But they've lived here for over five hundred years! They're as Irish as we are.

DEE: Without our potatoes, we'll starve!

AUSTIN: No, we live on an island. We'll eat fish. No one will starve.

REED: I curse the land! (*He stomps on the ground.*)

DEE: I curse the ground! (*She stomps on the ground.*)

ACT TWO 45

REED: Well, boyo?

AUSTIN: But I want to begin a new tradition of peace and brotherhood and mutual disarmament, and not be poisoned by generations of hate and bloodshed and—

REED: Shut yer festerin' gob! Who do ya' think ya' are, Sinead O'Connor? Next thing, you'll be cursin' the Pope!

AUSTIN: No. I curse the land. *(He stomps.)* I curse the ground. *(He stomps again.).* I curse the British bastards who own our fields. *(He stomps three times.)*

(They stomp the ground. Their stomping and high-stepping turns into Riverdance. DEE *and* REED *exit dancing.* AUSTIN *finishes, striking the Michael Flatley pose.)*

AUSTIN: And thus was born Bored of the Dance. Sure, and if you tolerated that, you'll tolerate our next act. He hails from Holland. Please bang your hands together for the impressionist Vincent Van Gogh.

(Cabaret drum roll/cymbal crash. REED *enters as* VINCENT VAN GOGH, *with a bloody bandage on his ear.)*

REED/VAN GOGH: Thank you very much. It's great to be here on this starry, starry night. My first impression will be of the legendary film actor, Mister Jimmy Stewart. *(He turns upstage to prepare, then back downstage for the impression.)* "Ah, I just want to say, it's a wonderful life."

(Audience gives an indifferent response)

REED/VAN GOGH: Don't patronize me. Obviously this world was never meant for one as beautiful as me, so I'm gonna cut to the chase here. I'm gonna finish up with my impression of a maniac who married a whore and chopped off his own ear. I think it might go a little something like this.

(He again turns upstage to prepare, then turns downstage holding a dismembered ear in his hand. The audience is unimpressed.)

REED/VAN GOGH: Thank you very much. You've been a completely indifferent audience. I'll be here all week. Don't forget to tip your waiters. I'll be opening up for this man. Please, give it up for the legendary impressionist—Mister Claude Monet!

(Cabaret drum roll/cymbal crash. REED exits. DEE enters as MONET wearing a gray beard, beret, and thick glasses. She speaks with a French accent.)

DEE/MONET: Zank you! Zank you! *(MONET is extremely overenthusiastic every time he says "Zank you".)* How 'bout zat Van Gogh, huh? Boy, I zink zat guy's a nut, but zat's just my impression. Zank you! Show me ze Monet! Zank you! Zank you! And now I would like to do Brigitte Bardot. But zen, who wouldn't like to do Brigitte Bardot, eh? Zank you! Zank you! And now, here's someone who needs no introduction, but zat will not stop me, Claude Monet, zank you. Pleez bang your knees togezzer for Monsieur Henri de Toulouse-Lautrec.

(She exits. Cabaret drum roll/cymbal crash. A spotlight picks up AUSTIN as TOULOUSE-LAUTREC. He's on his knees wearing a tiny costume where he puts his arms down the pant legs and his hands are used as feet. They are dressed with tap shoes.)

AUSTIN/TOULOUSE-LAUTREC: I would now like to do for you a short little impression—but zen what other kind could I do, eh? Zis is my impression of Samuel Morse, ze inventor of ze Telegraph.

(He taps out the dots and dashes of S-O-S with his feet, and does a short [!] tap number to hip-hop beat. Blackout. Lights up on REED wearing a beret and pencil-thin mustache. He plays an accordion.)

ACT TWO

REED: Bon soir, Madame et Monsieur. *(Sings)*
Of all Europeans ze Germans are worst
Zey started two world wars—ze Second and First
Wiz countenance dour
If zey're not in power
You bet your sweet strudel
A Kraut will be sour

Yet everybody hates ze French
Everybody hates ze French
To hate all ze Germans
Would make so much sense
Yet everybody hates ze French

Ze Russians were commies, ze Russians were reds
Their nuclear bomb-ies were aimed at our heads
But wiz perestroika
Everything's okey-doyka
But their economy's sunk
And you can bet zey're all drunk

Yet everybody hates ze French
Everybody hates ze French
To hate all ze Russians
And Germans makes sense
Yet everybody hates ze French

In England
Zey're living in ze past
In England
Zey separate by class
With teeth decayin'
And cows insane
Why don't zey pull ze sticks out of zeir ass?

Yet everybody hates ze French
Everybody hates ze French
To hate all ze English and Russians and Germans
Yes, that would make sense
Yet everybody hates ze French

(The next section is spoken in time with the music.)

I'm sure zat zey hate us for inventing mime
And we did lay down for Hitler in quite a short time
We consider snails food
And I admit it, we're rude
Our women don't shave
And, quite frankly, none of us bathe
Not to mention ze fact zat we play ze accordion
And worship Jerry Lewis
Frankly, now I see it, why....

(He sings again.)

Everybody hates ze French
Everybody hates ze French
Yes, now I see
Suddenly it makes sense
Why everybody hates ze French
(Spoken) Sing along!

(Sung) Everybody hates ze French
(Spoken) Oui, oui!
(Sung) Everybody hates ze French
(Spoken) Ha, ha, ha!
(Sung) Yes, now I see
I can hear you agree
Zat everybody hates ze French

We eat legs of froggies
We killed Lady Di
So everybody hates ze French
Oui! Oui!

(Blackout. Lights up on AUSTIN *seated in a* Masterpiece Theatre *chair, wearing a silk smoking jacket. He talks like Noel Coward.)*

AUSTIN/DISRAELI: Good evening, and welcome to *Ethnic Stereotypes*. I'm Benjamin Disraeli, Queen Victoria's favorite Prime Minister. I'm utterly delighted

ACT TWO 49

beyond measure to present to you my first guest this evening. He is the father of modern capitalism. From Kirkcaldy, Scotland, please give a big *Ethnic Stereotypes* welcome to Mister Adam Smith.

(REED *enters in a kilt and tam o'shanter to the sound of bagpipes.*)

REED/ADAM SMITH: *(He sings.)* Hoot man!
I am the father of modern economics known as laissez faire
Ironic then that Scotsmen are so tight
Beneath me kilt I'm not wearing underwear
If ya dinna believe me you're a bag a shite!

(REED *exits in disgust.* AUSTIN's *confused.*)

AUSTIN/DISRAELI: Did you understand a word he said? I don't understand economics either. Welcome back to *Ethnic Stereotypes*. Now, do you know what was the greatest dilemma I faced as England's first Jewish Prime Minister? Pork at half price. Ha-ha! I'm just kidding! Yes, I can see we're all comfortable with stereotypes, as long as one also admits our significant achievements. And in that regard, there is another group of people whose achievements we must also recognize and celebrate. The Muslims! Yes, I know what you're thinking: good heavens, where's he going with *this*? Now, I'm not talking about the handful of *(With extreme irony) incredibly* devout "Muslims" who go drinking in strip clubs the night before they commit atrocities, oh no. No, I'm talking about the other ninety-nine-point-nine percent of the world's Muslims who are no more screwed up than you and me. Because now more than ever, we here in the Western world mustn't forget that until very recently, the world was dominated by Muslim culture. And surely someday we're all going to have to learn to get along! You see the problem is that— *(His speech blends right*

into the song, just like Noel Coward and he begins to sing.)
—Everyone's afraid to talk
They stutter, stammer, or just gawk
No one wants to be the first to move
But if we're going to do this
We have to say, "Oh screw this!"
One look at Muslim history shows
They've got nothing to prove....

Do let's be frank about the Muslims
The time for speaking plainly has begun
They all bow down to Mecca
They're wonderful as heck-a
They really are an awful lot of fun

Their empire was Ottoman
They had an awful lot 'o men
Who were scientists, philosophers, and sages
Not all of them are Bedouin
They practiced modern medicine
When the western world was still in the Dark Ages

So do let's be frank about the Muslims
Yes, I know they seem exotic to a foreigner
But Muslim men and women
Invented coffee up in Yemen
Blame them for every Starbucks on your corner

Now there were many popes
Who were absolutely dopes
Who I'd really like to take and shake and throttle
Because they kept down Greek philosophy
But fortunately for you and me
A Muslim man translated
A lotta Aristotle

So do let's be frank about the Muslims
They brought Mohammed right up to the mountain
They gave us algebra, and that's not all

ACT TWO

The zero and the Taj Mahal
They also gave us jihad, but who's countin'?
Even if you all skipped college
You really must acknowledge
That they did it all before us and did it well
A favor you'll be doin' me
When you admit they're just like you and me
Even though their names are
(Spoken) impossible to spell quite frankly I don't know how they do it actually much less pronounce them I mean really! *(He's almost unintelligible by the end)* Never mind. *(Resumes singing)*
Do let's be frank about the Muslims
Just give those swarthy warriors their due
They all deserve some credit
Jews and Christians all have said it
They said, do let's give those towel-heads their due!
(Spoken) And I totally agree. Thank you very much, and good night!

(Blackout. The Unsung Song music starts. Lights up on DEE*)*

DEE: What about the unsung restaurant employees who actually do wash their hands before they touch your food? And what about that guy, you know, he wrote all those pretty sonnets and then he wrote that play Hamlet? What's that guy's name? Nobody knows. And what about that guy who chopped down the cherry tree and then became our first President? Nobody knows his name, do they? Well, this is for them—*The Unsung Song.*

(Music has become more insistent but is cut off abruptly once more.)

COMPUTER VOICE: Loading Disk Number Six.

DEE: Wait! I thought I was going to get to sing the song!

COMPUTER VOICE: You know I would never prevent you from singing *The Unsung Song*.

DEE: Good, because I'm not leaving this stage until I sing this song.

COMPUTER VOICE: By the way, you look great. Have you lost weight?

DEE: How patronizing. *(Beat)* Really?

COMPUTER VOICE: Oh yes. You definitely have lost weight. You should go backstage and look in the mirror.

(DEE *starts to exit. Blackout. She yells, tricked.*)

DEE: Wait!

COMPUTER VOICE: Ha ha ha ha ha.

THE INFORMATION AGE

(*Suddenly the* COMPUTER VOICE *is gone and we hear* AUSTIN's *amplified voice.*)

AUSTIN: Ha, ha, ha, ha, ha! Loading disk number six. Chapter Six. The Information—wait, have we lost the computer effect? Chapter Six—we have. *(He steps onstage from the wings. He speaks into a handheld mic and looks up to the booth.)* Could you please turn the.... *(His voice is now replaced by the normal* COMPUTER VOICE*)* ... computer effect back on? Oh, there it is. Thank you. *(Resuming)* Chapter Six. The Information Age. The Church is intolerant and the world is run by a handful of wealthy white men.

(REED *and* DEE *have entered upstage of* AUSTIN *and are staring at him.*)

AUSTIN: *(Computer voice)* They're right behind me, aren't they?

ACT TWO 53

REED: *(He takes the microphone from* AUSTIN.*)* Well, thank you very much, Computer Boy. I think Dee and I can take it from here.

DEE: That is terrible!

AUSTIN: Okay, I apologize.

REED: Good.

DEE: You should.

AUSTIN: I'm very very sorry I got caught.

REED & DEE: What?!

AUSTIN: Fine! I was controlling the whole thing and now you guys can do whatever you want. But I was trying to do the right thing.

DEE: The right thing?

AUSTIN: I was trying to maintain the lie.

DEE: What lie?

AUSTIN: The *big* lie! I was doing it for them! I was trying to maintain the big lie we've all been taught and we're all supposed to believe, that everything important in history was done by a straight, right-handed, white man. *That* lie. *(To audience)* Right? *(He starts to go but stops because the audience is quiet.)*

REED: Sounds to me like there's a lot of left-handed lesbians of color out there.

*(*REED *and* DEE *hold their left fists in the air as a sign of solidarity.* AUSTIN *stares at the audience in disdain.)*

AUSTIN: You're so P C. *(He exits.)*

DEE: I don't believe him!

REED: It's okay, it's an opportunity! What have you wanted to cover that Austin wouldn't let you do?

DEE: *The Unsung Song!*

REED: Great.

DEE: Mamie Eisenhower!

REED: Fantastic.

(DEE *gets an idea and exits.*)

REED: And now, finally, ladies and gentlemen, a song about women. You know, there have been so many important women throughout the history of Western Civilization. Florence Nightingale, Virginia Woolf, Richard Simmons, Ally McBeal, I could go on and on. But rather than do a song about a specific woman, this number is about the single invention that….

(DEE *has dashed on carrying the Genghis Khan outfit and moustache and starts putting it on* REED.)

REED: Thank you. And—what's this?

DEE: You said I could do what I wanted to do.

REED: You can. But I haven't even started mine yet. And I told you before, I do not want to sing the Genghis Khan Love Ballad.

DEE: Don't worry, it's better than that.

(*She pushes her arms behind the up-center drop and* AUSTIN *leaps on from the other side. He's dressed as* ADOLF HITLER.)

DEE: It's a duet. Come here. I finally figured it out. The Great Lesson of Western Civilization is that those who forget the past are doomed to repeat it. These two are the most evil figures of western civilization and they bookend the millennium. Genghis Khan. Charlie Chaplin. Sing!

(*Piano introduction is heard.* DEE *exits.*)

AUSTIN/HITLER: I thought I was …

REED/KHAN: I thought you were, too.

(*The music has begun, so they're forced to sing.*)

ACT TWO

REED/KHAN:
Can't believe that we have to sing this song

AUSTIN/HITLER:
Although we've started now it still feels wrong

REED/KHAN: But we're stuck

AUSTIN/HITLER: What the hell

BOTH: How will we get through the Hitler/Khan duet?

REED/KHAN: Every show has to have a song like this

AUSTIN/HITLER:
Fine by me, long as we don't have to kiss

REED/KHAN: What to do?

AUSTIN/HITLER: Me and you

BOTH: Have no choice but sing the Hitler/Khan duet
Once again I've been taken by surprise
Why portray men we all cannot abide?
Hold me close. I fear we'll be misunderstood
Nothing that they did was good
At least until the day they died

Take a stand, fight against all evil men
We demand, don't let their kind rise again
No regret
Don't forget
We don't want another Hitler/Khan duet

(They shrug and give each other a big smooch. Blackout. Night state. Space music fades in and they all enter dressed as astronauts singing harmony to the tune of Four Norsemen of the Apocalypse—*but at half-tempo.)*

ALL: We are the three spacemen in the Apollo ship
We're hoping Tang will give us sponsorship
Three spacemen in the Apollo ship
Moon, moon, moon…

(They're wearing various inappropriately recycled costumes from earlier in the show. AUSTIN *wears a Viking helmet.* REED *wears the bedpan on his head as a helmet. They slowly enter, close together, as if they are floating in space.* DEE *wears the Helen Keller outfit [without the cane and glasses] to become* MAMIE EISENHOWER *[although her voice is pure* KATHARINE HEPBURN*]. All three speak into their hands and pinch their noses, muffling their voices to make them sound like spacemen on microphones.)*

AUSTIN/NEIL ARMSTRONG: Mission Control, this is Apollo 11. We are ready for separation. Over. Initiating separation. Over.

REED/MICHAEL COLLINS: Firing separation rockets. Over.

(They reveal super-soaker squirt guns and fire their "rockets" at the audience, as AUSTIN *and* DEE *separate from* REED. AUSTIN *and* DEE *head to the center of the stage.* REED *heads to the other side of the stage, as the audience screams at being squirted.)*

AUSTIN/ARMSTRONG: In space, no one can hear you scream.

DEE/MAMIE: We'd like to thank President Nixon for his good wishes. And my husband Dwight was proud to have him serve as his Vice-President. Over.

REED/COLLINS: Commander, I'm a little confused as to why Mamie Eisenhower is on this Mission with us. Over.

AUSTIN/ARMSTRONG: Frankly, I think we all are. Over.

DEE/MAMIE: And I'm a little confused as to why we keep saying "over", over and over. Over.

AUSTIN/ARMSTRONG: Ten-four. We're over saying "over", over and over. Over.

ACT TWO

REED/COLLINS: I'm also a little confused as to why Mamie Eisenhower sounds exactly like Katharine Hepburn.

DEE/HEPBURN: Oh, shut up you old poop.

AUSTIN/ARMSTRONG: Tranquility base here. The Eagle has landed.

(AUSTIN *and* DEE *mime landing on the moon, then make a caw-caw bird sound in unison.*)

AUSTIN/ARMSTRONG: We are stepping out onto the surface of the moon. This is one small step for man....

DEE/MAMIE: ...but nonetheless rather difficult in orthopedic shoes.

REED/COLLINS: Commander, as long as we're out here, we may as well take this opportunity to get the people in back [in the balcony] who thought they were safe.

(*They make their way toward the back of the theater and squirt the audience.*)

REED/COLLINS: You know, Commander, as I look around here I think I have the answer to that age-old question.

AUSTIN/ARMSTRONG: What's that?

REED/COLLINS: Absolutely no signs of intelligent life out here.

DEE/MAMIE: Spray it again, Sam.

(*They all spray the audience again.*)

REED/COLLINS: Austin, we have—I mean Houston, we have a problem.

AUSTIN/ARMSTRONG: You mean that Mamie can't decide if she's Katharine Hepburn or Humphrey Bogart? That problem?

REED/COLLINS: Well, that, but also there seems to be a very strange smell here in outer space. Of course, that could be the bedpan on my head.

DEE/MAMIE: That's not a bedpan. That's a space helmet. You've changed its context so you've changed its function. *(She triumphantly puts both arms up in the air.)* I've got a chicken in my pants.

REED/COLLINS: Mamie, shut the hell up!

(REED *and* AUSTIN *point their squirt guns at* DEE, *who retreats to the front row of the audience. She sits on the lap of an audience member for protection.)*

REED/COLLINS: And quit making out with the aliens.

(DEE *suddenly hops off the man's lap.)*

DEE/MAMIE: He's got a chicken in his pants!

AUSTIN/ARMSTRONG: And he's not afraid to use it.

REED/COLLINS: I think the biggest problem is that no one can understand a word we're saying 'cause we're covering our mouths and pinching our noses.

AUSTIN/ARMSTRONG: Sorry, I didn't get that. You're covering your mouth and pinching your nose. Say again, over.

REED/COLLINS: Screw it.

(To get back up onstage, DEE *lies on the stage, waving and putting her arms and legs in the air.)*

AUSTIN/ARMSTRONG: Good lord. Mamie's gone into free fall. Mamie, it's time to go. You plant your little flag and light this candle.

(DEE *pulls out a small American flag and hands it to a woman in the front row.)*

DEE/MAMIE: Here. Shove that in your crater.

AUSTIN/ARMSTRONG: Mission control, we are leaving the moon's surface. So I guess we'd better fire rockets.

ACT TWO 59

(They squirt the crowd one final time.)

AUSTIN/ARMSTRONG: Believe it or not, we came in peace for all mankind.

REED/COLLINS: And womenkind.

DEE/MAMIE: Aboard the African Queen.

REED/COLLINS: Commander, this evening I feel just like John Glenn.

AUSTIN/ARMSTRONG: How's that?

REED/COLLINS: I am getting way too old for this crap.

AUSTIN/ARMSTRONG: Mission control, we're headed home.

(They "float" off in slow motion, DEE first followed by AUSTIN and REED, singing in harmony as they go.)

ALL: *(Sung)* Three spacemen in the Apollo ship!

(The lights shift as DEE enters as Albert Einstein with gray fright wig and mustache. She wears silly glasses with eyes on springs.)

DEE/EINSTEIN: Und zis iz ze room vere ve make ze bombs, und ze rockets, und ze nuclear mizziles. Izn't it funny zat a voman dizcovers radioactivity and uses it to cure disease, vile men use it to build bombs? Vell, not funny ha-ha, funny total global deztruction. Unt since zis show needs a big finish, I am now going to blow you all to smithereens. Boom!

(AUSTIN enters dressed similarly, but without the goofy glasses.)

AUSTIN/OPPENHEIMER: Professor! Professor! I have a question—

DEE/EINSTEIN: *(Startled by AUSTIN's entrance; her eyes dance crazily.)* My eyes betray me!

AUSTIN/OPPENHEIMER: Professor, I have a question to ask of you.

DEE/EINSTEIN: Vait vun second. You have stolen my German accent.

AUSTIN/OPPENHEIMER: No, zis iz my German accent. I am Docter Robert Oppenheimer.

DEE/EINSTEIN: He vuz American!

AUSTIN/OPPENHEIMER: *(Referring to the audience)* Ja, but zey don't know zis, so who cares....

DEE/EINSTEIN: Oh! Zat is terrible! *(She jumps up and down in outrage, and one of her eyes falls off its spring. To the audience)* I'm okay. *(She finds where it went, then points off in the other direction.)*

DEE/EINSTEIN: Look, it's Salman Rushdie!

(When AUSTIN looks away, she snatches the eye off the floor. She tries unsuccessfully to put it back on the spring.)

AUSTIN/OPPENHEIMER: I could have told you zat vould happen. I mean, I'm no rocket scientist, but...if you play viz it, it'll fall off.

DEE/EINSTEIN: Oh! You are a dirty.... *(She holds the eye way out to the side.)* You don't know vere to look, do you?

AUSTIN/OPPENHEIMER: No, I don't....

(She puts the eye on the back of her head.)

DEE/EINSTEIN: Eye caramba! Hey, do you know who my favorite person is?

AUSTIN/OPPENHEIMER: No, who?

DEE/EINSTEIN: Mamie Eyesenhower!

AUSTIN/OPPENHEIMER: I uh...I guess your muzzer vas right.

DEE/EINSTEIN: Ja. It's alvays funny till somebody loses an eye.

ACT TWO

AUSTIN/OPPENHEIMER: Listen—ve must do something about ze cloning.

DEE: We need to stop it by blowing it up!

AUSTIN: No. Ve need to cover ze Scotsman who perfected ze art of—

(REED *leaps out from backstage, again dressed in his Scottish outfit.*)

REED: Did someone say, "Scotsman"?

(*Cue bagpipes.* REED *sings to the tune of* Scotland the Brave.)

REED/SCOTS CLONER:
I cloned a sheep named Dolly
Now I'm a famous Scot, by golly
Soon I'll be cloning people for human parts

I'm sick from eating haggis
But I've learned how great a shag is
It gives me joy, but I'm a very baaaaaaaad boy!
(*Spoken*) Thank ye!

(*During the song,* AUSTIN *and* DEE *throw out one inflatable sheep, then two, then four, six, etc. Plus one inflatable pig, which* AUSTIN *accidentally-on-purpose throws over* REED *and into the front row.* AUSTIN *comes on to help clear up.* REED *gestures for the pig to be thrown back up onstage. When it is, he holds it up to show that it doesn't match.*)

AUSTIN: (*To the person who threw it back onstage*) What did you do?

(REED *picks up one of the inflatable sheep, which is almost entirely deflated.*)

REED: She must have been extremely popular with the laddies.

AUSTIN: Aye. An embraceable ewe.

REED: Aye.

(DEE *dashes on.* AUSTIN *strikes some sheep.*)

DEE: Yes! This is what I was talking about earlier! All you need is love. The love between a Scotsman and his sheep.

AUSTIN: No...

REED: Dee, if we've learned anything at all tonight, it's that love is dangerous.

(*Doo-wop piano strikes up.*)

AUSTIN: Haven't you been paying attention?

DEE: *(Referring to the audience)* As much as they have.

(REED *strikes the rest of the sheep.* AUSTIN *sings.*)

AUSTIN: Ferdinand loved Imelda
Bought her a lot of shoes
Adolf loved Eva
You know what he tried to do
Romeo loved Juliet
More than a priceless gem
Henry the Eighth loved all of his wives
Look what happened to them

ALL: Ain't it crazy how love works
Ain't it crazy how love works

AUSTIN: Hinckley loved Jodie
Thought he'd give romance a shot
Nobody loved Cambodia
More than its leader Pol Pot
Jesus said that loving thy neighbor
Is the name of the game
Some folks love Jesus so much
They kill people in his name

ALL: Ain't it crazy how love works
Ain't it crazy how love works

AUSTIN: When a woman says I love you
There's never a proper response

ACT TWO 63

When a man says I love you
You know what he really wants—
And wants and wants and wants and wants and wants!

(AUSTIN *thrusts his pelvis until he notices the others shaking their heads in disgust. He fans his face to cool off and continues.*)

AUSTIN: The Wallendas loved flying
Ended up taking a fall
O J loved Nicole so much
He never killed her at all
Dodi loved Diana
Howard Hughes loved all of his wealth

ALL: If you look at the way all these people end up
You can see love is bad for your health
Ain't it crazy how love works
Ain't it crazy how love works

AUSTIN: Jimmy Hoffa loved the Teamsters so much
He went on a permanent strike

ALL: Maybe it's safer for everyone
To only go falling in like
Ain't it crazy how love works
Ain't it crazy how love works

(*Blackout. Unsung Song music starts again. Lights up on* DEE.)

DEE: Everybody wears Levi jeans, but nobody knows the name of the man who invented them. Or what about _____ the Infidel? (*She says the name of the man she picked on earlier in the Torquemada scene.*) Doesn't he deserve a song? Look at him. Of course he does. He needs a new wardrobe. And a hair cut. This is for him, for _____, and for all of history's unsung heroes. Finally, the *Unsung Song*!

(DEE *sings the first note of the song then stops.*)

DEE: Wait a second. *That's* the Great Lesson of Western Civilization. Stop the music!

(*The music peters out.* AUSTIN *and* REED *have drifted on.*)

AUSTIN: What's going on?

REED: Of course! It took a woman to finally figure it out!

AUSTIN: Wait—why should we believe her?

DEE: Because I've got a chicken in my pants! Look, history repeats itself. There's always another explorer and inventor. More war and prejudice. Back then we had Alexander the Fabulous.

REED: Now, Ellen Degeneres!

DEE: Exactly! Back then we had war between Jews and Arabs.

AUSTIN: Now, we have war between Jews and Arabs.

AUSTIN/REED: Exactly!

DEE: And the Church is still intolerant and the world will be run….

ALL: …by a handful of wealthy white men!

(*Guitar strums the intro to the final song.*)

DEE: Like Oprah!

AUSTIN & REED: Exactly!

(DEE *sings.*)

DEE: It's not a roller coaster
More like a ferris wheel
We're on a ride that'll never end

REED: It's deja vu all over again

AUSTIN: Another great invention
Another wonder cure
Another brand-new amazing trend

ACT TWO

REED: It's deja vu all over again
Gotta do it, nothing to it
Everybody deja vu it

ALL: Deja vu

AUSTIN: If it happened before

ALL: Deja vu

REED: It'll happen some more

ALL: Deja vu
You can remember when
It's deja vu all over again

REED & AUSTIN: *(Sung)* It's deja vu all over again

AUSTIN: It's like a White House scandal
Or a bowl of chili beans
They keep repeating without an end

REED & DEE: It's deja vu all over again

REED: Gotta swing it, gotta wing it
C'mon everybody sing it

ALL: Deja vu

AUSTIN: If it happened before

ALL: Deja vu

REED: It'll happen some more

ALL: Deja vu
You can remember when
It's deja vu all over again

If you've seen this show before
Or you think the jokes aren't new
If you've seen this show before
I'm having deja vu!

So now the show is over
There's only one thing wrong
This is a really repetitive song—

ALL: It's deja vu all over again
Deja vu
If it happened before
Deja vu
It'll happen some more
Deja vu
If it happened before
Deja vu
It'll happen some more
Deja vu
You can remember when
It's deja vu all over again!
(Spoken) History!!

(Blackout. Bows)

THE END

www.ingramcontent.com/pod-product-compliance
Lightning Source LLC
Chambersburg PA
CBHW071748040426
42446CB00012B/2497